Rita F. Snowden is widely   e
author of more than sixty b   r
years at business she traine   ....and
Methodist Church, serving   ....ioneer country areas
before moving to the largest ...y for several years of social work
during an economic depression.

Miss Snowden has served the world Church, beyond her own
denomination, with regular broadcasting commitments. She has
written and spoken in Britain, Canada, the United States, in
Australia, and in Tonga at the invitation of Queen Salote. She
has represented her church at the World Methodist Conference
in Oxford; later being elected the first woman Vice-President of
the New Zealand Methodist Church, and President of its
Deaconess Association. She has served as an Honorary Vice-
President of the New Zealand Women Writers' Society, is a
Fellow of the International Institute of Art and Letters, and a
member of P.E.N.

Miss Snowden has been honoured by the award of the Order
of the British Empire, and by the citation of "The Upper Room"
in America.

Her most recent books are *Prayers for Busy People, Christianity
Close to Life, Bedtime Stories and Prayers* (for children), *I Believe
Here and Now, Discoveries That Delight, Further Good News, Con-
tinually Aware, Good Company, Prayers in Large Print* and *Like
Wind on the Grasses*.

Books by the same author
available in Fount Paperbacks

Bedtime Stories and Prayers
(for children)
Continually Aware
Discoveries That Delight
Further Good News
Good Company
I Believe Here and Now
Like Wind on The Grasses
More Prayers for Women
Prayers in Large Print
A Woman's Book of Prayers

Rita Snowden also edited
In the Hands of God
by William Barclay

Rita Snowden

SECRETS

Collins
FOUNT PAPERBACKS

First published in Great Britain in 1986
by Fount Paperbacks, London

Copyright © Rita F. Snowden 1986

Made and printed in Great Britain by
William Collins Sons & Co. Ltd, Glasgow

With happy thoughts
of my friend
Dora Hessell

Contents

Preface

Of my many books finding a place on my home shelves, and on countless others the world round, there is no other quite like this. I've been writing it for years – as one writes an early diary for no other eyes, or as a private knot of words to go under one's pillow.

But the time comes when it could be a pleasure to share. I have many fine friends, who over the years have read my books, and written me letters about them. To these I want to say: "Don't take fright when you find the form in which this one appears – you will find it as easy to read, once you get going, as anything you've ever read. And, I hope, as rewarding."

You might, by now, have a treasurable collection of your own, that you never show to anyone. Or this might set you off.

We are all, of course, private persons – however public our daily service. We are not obliged to share – though something might well be added to life if we decide to do so.

We'll see!

R. F. S.

Country Born

I was cradled in the country
to the sweet choreography of winds
and the humble breath of clover.
My earliest coins dandelions,
close companions, birds,
adventures, along the paths feet sought out.

My songs came from the river,
and rain upon the roof,
motley from the leaves, at the Autumn of the year.
Winter's timely skill
set jewels for my waking,
and chiselled sharp at night a myriad stars.

In Spring – seed surrendered,
multiplied in being spent –
hope took on stalk and ear.
Summer's legacy of leafy boughs
served imagination –
then a school-bell rang, and a spire arose.

So, in body, mind and spirit
I was rich –
before ever a tall city could gather me in.

Childhood

Once . . .
Though I was but seven,
it was a wonder
right out of heaven
to gather mushrooms
at dawn's first light –
in neat fairy rings,
a gift of the night.

In A Loved
Country School

Small children still skip in diamond sunlight
till the loud throaty bell gathers them in
to their known desks to read and write.

Miss Dansey directs all silence and sound,
ever kindly, each questioner welcomed –
heads down, as the old clock ticks round.

But how many will plough, hope, and grow corn,
and not choose a loud city's pollution,
for this sweet air where we were born?

Growing Up

Laughter soon enlarged my landscape –
quickened my hearing, my sight,
refreshed my spirit's colours,
bringing each day new delight.

At first, I prayed to be rich –
but that has now long ended –
since work, leisure, joy and love
richly my heart befriended.

And The Years Pass

A first loved teacher is remembered long,
an early lark remains a sightless song,
manhood breaks a lad's "flute" for speech made new,
four living seasons lead each full year through,
whilst finer than shrubs foliate in May,
Discovery makes beautiful our common way.

Some Senses Withheld

Five senses I have –
Yet all too few they are:
I cannot hear the crisp crack of dawn;
nor record the surprise of the crocus
to find herself garbed in gold;
I cannot smell or taste exactly
the rain-drop's heart given to the earth;
nor share the green beetle's ecstasy
as he runs up the tall grass-stalk.

I would like to know the joke
when the early star winks;
and the maternal mood of the old mother cow
calmly chewing her cud in the velvety dusk;
the music scale of the river
running over gravel, all through the night;
and there are the secret steps of the dew
in my garden at dawn, that allow jeweller's tricks
on cobwebs when the spider isn't looking.

Bread On The Table

Here, morning breaks as the world's first morning;
the lark on high spills her silver coins of song.
We of the earth cannot live by bread alone,
nor can we live without it long.
So a furrow is turned by honest plough,
and good seed flung into the earth,
rain follows sun in slender spears
till thin tassels spring to birth.

Nothing of God's giving is so golden crusted,
nothing so sweet to taste and need as bread,
save that our brother afar faints for it –
bread tilled for, sown and harvested.
We would not begrudge nectar to the tipsy bee
winging from flower to flower the long day through
our grievous fault is that we withhold this hour
bread from our brother who knows hunger too.

One Full Autumn Day

Leisure led my feet up a distant hill,
to a poplar Midas gold,
leaves spiralling down at will.
I could only stand silent,
soon aware of sky and birds.
Now – these many rich years on –
I still find myself wond'ring:
But how can I put all this into words?

The Lake's Mirror

This is a generous day
    when each brown duck swims double,
each pine punctures the sky
    and pierces the lake's heart,
as I meander by.

Here a child in a red coat
    near the edge,
has a playmate in a red coat, pellucid,
where the elements earth, air and water
    peacefully float.

A Night At My Grandparents'

This old house – with all asleep but me –
never quite forgets that it was trees
once, under wide skies, breathing free,
each season answering each breeze,
speaking now through an old-age creak.

Dear wooden house, let me give you praise
for your tall, generous roof by night,
and your open windows and doors, through days
welcoming in sun's sweet light,
and a breeze through arpeggios of leaves.

How many have been born in this place,
I wonder now as I lie awake;
how many grown to mind and soul space
here, over the years, to face and shake
things, and to know life's meed of laughter?

Praise!

I find much joy in simple things –
sun's early shafts on the still cool grass,
a wash, and a kettle that sings,
archipelagos of clouds that pass
over trees tenanted by soft winds.

Golden nut-brown toast with marmalade,
a bell calling little ones to school,
changing leaf-patterns in the blue shade,
a fluting blackbird in evening's cool,
and a skein of duck flying homeward.

So I bring my canticle of praise
for these, and my room with lamp at dusk,
for sweet rest after absorbing days,
and many a kernel in the husk
of printed books gathered through the years!

A Letter In Reply

Dear Snail:
    You came before my usual morning mail
    and left a letter on my doorstep,
    scrawled in silver ink, as always,
    to tell me that my lettuces were gone –
    my tender ones, pride of my heart;
    and now I am bereft.

    You hadn't need to write –
    I'd have known it in time, I've had a screed
    from you before – in the same scrawl,
    in the same ink. Don't write again
    unless you have some better news –
    just now I am bereft.

Night Flight Overhead

Night – and I lie in the gentle dark,
    about to pull a dream over my head;
till your pulsing-zooming presence sets a prayer
    on my lips: "God speed you!"
And I stir to wonder what this hour means to you –
    night flight for London half a world away.
For you the casual competence of aircrew, care of
    hostesses?
Men, women and children, here altogether – as many, as varied
    as any village breathing air.
Some, on studies bent? Some, to feel for
    the world's pocketbook?
Some, knowingly sophisticated, seeking fortunes
    of the heart?

In your metal miracle aloft, you press your way forward
    as surely as migrating birds –
to lay hold of a new dimension – as those who launch
    into immortality –
The Past all behind, the Future all before!

Among The Hills

I sit sun-blessed, reading my map –
pleasantly sprawled from my car apart;
though no cartographer's spell
is a match for the map in my heart.

That lone traveller in far off days
marked down this distance from home;
neatly named forests and streams
for those of us unborn, who would come.

Now, thanks to his adventuring heart
and all that he managed to find,
I rejoice in river and range –
"line" and "caterpillar" in his mind.

Others later, brought green grasses
to this light wind whispering by,
and set cattle and sheep on these hills
shouldering the sky.

Modern Decibels

Once, each day entered
  without knocking,
though childhood cherished
  its own sounds –
water running over
  grey gravel,
bird chatter in tall trees
  out of bounds.

When sun finished
  popping gorse-pods,
and larks surrendered hold
  on the blue,
night summoned her cicada
  orchestra,
with sleep before the concert
  was through.

Now, day enters with
  grating gears,
While transistors bawl
  threatening ills;
and jets rip the selvedge
  off the sky,
above a stutter of pneumatic
  drills!

Fidelity Of Friends

Time's pupil,
God lends me friends with honest hearts,
and sudden laughter,
blessed with senses five –
and rich experience
lacking in apple-tree Eden.

Life is shared –
as new horizons break for each –
not where earth meets sky –
but where hearts reach out
in doubt or dance,
depending on Faith, Hope and Love!

For Homecoming

Plant a sunflower by my gate
with a wise, golden face,
that when I come home late
I may know her grace.

Tired of limb and mind
in the great world's employ,
I shall there sense
the primacy of joy!

Country Respite

Hours out of doors are now vanishing
   like fluff of a dandelion clock,
cicadas singing the requiem of Summer;
   my garnering to carry into Autumn
a great sheaf of lovely things.
For the days when blunt rain falls,
   friendly pines groan
and no living thing, meanwhile, is on
   speaking terms with the sun.

But in the country here, there is always
   a late valley train
chuffing its slender way beyond the
   range of hearing,
a dog turning in his guardianship, as I
   latch the door for the fire,
and a good, long read – pausing now and again
   to crack a word
to get at its sweet kernel.

A Solitary

Poised high on a branch of advantage against the sky,
the kingfisher watches acutely each fish and fly
moving within pool and weed –
then shows himself fashioned of sapphire speed.

Royally named, who first brought him to Court?
And which king acknowledged his instant sport?
A match for a bowman of ancient skill, a bullet of blue
piercing Earth's air and water through!

Joy Of Marigolds

Gold in the sun, each holding its face
rounded as a halo of grace
for eyes above some lowly task,
needing a glimpse of Paradise!

Named for Mary-of-Nazareth's hours,
brought from afar, these simple flowers,
in holds of ships with tall sails set,
moving with ease into our lives.

And such values, I find, such love
raises us gently above
the greedy gain of this brash age
with its coins and columns added up!

Tall Against The Sky

A tree trusts to no calendar, only the season's
     sap,
to no alarm clock, sleeping late, rising
     early,
its obedience to life is a grace no man
     knows;
tender in Spring's green, adventurous in
     Summer,
Autumn's felicities clothed in generous
     gold,
Winter's spare gift filigreed against the
     sky.

Who can remember his first tree – looked-up-into,
     loved?
Rocks covet only a shallow covering of
     lichen,
but a tree spells out clearly the Creator's
     purpose –
a ministry in scent and shade, strength and
     usefulness,
rain trickling into the thirsty earth
     waiting,
fields, gardens, hills saved from aridity and
     erosion
with a family house raised from fine-grained
     timber.

He who plants a tree, lends human aid to God's
purpose,
a wonder each season renewed for those who look
on it;
he plants a friend of sun, wind and
sky,
a strong shimmering beauty towering
high,
a kindness for creatures, as for his fellow
men,
he incarnates green thoughts born with the birth
of Time
and on-going generations will bless
him!

From Our Loved Home "West Hills"

Outside tonight, the rainstorm knuckles our
               panes,
but once indoors, embracing peace
               gains
its place against the elements.

From many lands this room has its
               grace,
brought by others to this quiet
               place,
fashioned shapes, colours, textures, clays.

Visible still, old woodsmen say, are
               hints
of loveliness the tree knew in life,
               tints
of the fire we rejoice in now.

With music, are books shoulder to
               shoulder,
pictures, and bright copper kettle
               older
than all else in hospitality.

Wherever you are, good craftsmen
               tonight,
know that we handle with thanks and
               delight
what your hearts and your hands have made.

Miracle Sleep

Each night's sleep is a *Nunc Dimittis*,*
said Poet John Donne** after long thought.
It covers one over completely, from entry
into this world, bringing its own good gifts.
Gently given, unmatched is this miracle –
alike to babe and baldhead,
a gracious expression of God's caring –
never say: "I will not accept a gift I do not understand!"

  * Luke 2:25–30
** John Donne 1573–1631

As I Enter To Worship

Here, I allow the Good News – God's enduring Mercy
promised by the prophets,
set to song by the psalmists,
illumined by the gospel scribes,
gloriously fulfilled in His Son –
gladly and wholly to command my heart's assent!

Two Lost Sons

Pig's-wash of wild husks was one's bread,
with poor rags to cover his back,
while his brother ate well, and wore
fine linen with a bright gold thread:
but both were prodigals – apart,
one, in the sad "far country",
one, at home, dark with resentment
eating deep into his heart.

Luke 15:11–32; Authorised Version

This Is The Hour!
(Communion)

This is the hour of the Broken Bread,
    the hour of the Outpoured Wine –
a fellowship of loving Faith
    become especially mine.
Whilst I make a vow at this Table spread,
    trusting little in human worth –
Rather in the Living Mercy of Christ --
    Risen Triumphant in this very Earth!

With Bowed Head

This world around, I have crossed many doorways –
  to homes, prisons, palaces, places of worship –
But none like this which gives me entry into the
  birth-place of our Lord –
built over a humble spot, here in Bethlehem's Church
  of the Nativity

For centuries, its arched height opened impressively –
  till straying beasts came, and infidels riding proudly.
Then those who cared lovingly, re-made this
  doorway – low-arched, and of hand-hewn stone.
So now, all of us of the Faith who would enter, fittingly come
  with bowed head – remembering that *In the fulness
  of Time, God sent forth His Son, made of a woman . . .
  to redeem.**

* Galatians 4:4–5; Authorized Version

Peter Remembers

He came striding along the water's edge,
   clothed in man's five senses.
   The boats beached, I was mending snagged nets,
   scaly, and deep-sea washed.
   And soon – I was snatching up cloak and sandals
   ready to walk the world with Him.

I never met another like Him –
   as straight in thought as in manly stance,
   wind in His hair, kissing His cheek,
   His eyes going straight to the point.
   Again and again, my words tumbled each other,
   but there was no hiding secrets from Him.

Days passed in dusty towns, the sick clamouring –
   nights under the stars, as we camped,
   so robust He was, so sure, He kept turning
   life's water into wine.
   Mothers and children sought Him, at ease,
   along with lepers, and the learned.

My fisherman's eyes were half-shut, limited –
   and there came a week I could never have guessed.
   Each of His words sadly distorted – spelling out
   the dark Garden, circled thorn and death.
   One of our company grasped in palm, and heart,
   coins as terrible as thirty suns blazing.

And we all scattered, to follow afar off –
    caught in madness, committed to grief.
    Seeking comfort at a fire of coals,
    a servant girl threw a noose of words about my neck.
    Pilate – so human his judgement – faltered,
    washed his hands – a dust-bowl in his heart.

And suddenly there was a Cross to be carried
    up a cruel hill, crowds jeering –
    He was King still, though covered now in sweat.
    The tumult echoing up the walled street
    waned only when He hung there stark against the sky –
    a thin uncertain company standing by.

The cruel day's end brought His body down – broken, limp;
    each who dared His friendship
    fashioning his own silent epitaph;
    staggering bewilderment and grief
    slammed doors for safety; the dank grave
    holding His body.

Spices weigh heavy when the heart is numb –
    but the women, purposeful, slipped out early
    ere the sun's arrows were laid across the grass;
    so were first to hear a step – and a name spoken;
    before John and I could come running
    to find the stone rolled away.

Let soldiers argue, and those they serve –
    there was no shadow on that dawn.
    I heard that Voice again – that very Voice,
    bereft of love no longer – broken out of Death!
    And I knew what I must do, and where
    through all the world, my stumbling feet must take me!

The First Easter News!

They told it,
not in some safe, distant place
where nobody had yet heard –
but in that very city
where men had shouted hoarsely,
"Crucify Him! Crucify Him!"

They told it,
not after weeks, years
when passion had cooled – but at once,
within Pilate's hearing,
and of all who judged, soldiered, shouted,
involved in that dastardly deed.

They told it,
confidently believing –
ran, meeting their Living Lord in the way –
a personal confrontation
that, more than an empty tomb reported,
changed the world!

They told it,
who had scattered in fear,
guilty of denial at a servant's word,
hiding behind shut doors,
sharing stuttering doubt –
transformed now marvellously,
men of mighty courage!

Easter Banners

Hang out your hallelujahs!
The Tomb is open,
the Roman Guard gone,
Death defeated!
The Man of Life walks again,
comforting the troubled,
healing the sick,
forgiving sinners,
spreading His Gospel through the lips
and lives of men made new!

The World's Need Of Bread

The first bread I tasted came from my mother's
                              oven,
gold-crusted, sweetest of the gifts of
                              earth,
made from the best flour, from the best
                              grain
grown in the sun-blessed countryside that gave
                              me birth.

Working till the shadows lengthened at
                              night,
in the mill by the stream I came to love as
                              my own,
the miller white in sacramental dust,
                              fulfilling
the hope with which the seed had been
                              sown.

Now, with each passing day in this hungry world,
                              comes bread –
from soil tilled, seed sown, and tended with
                              care,
rain and sun bringing us a gift beyond
                              price,
given us, that we might daily learn to
                              share.

Pietà

Shafts of morning light led me from
    Rome's surging streets
into St Peter's holy silence,
to stand before Michelangelo's
    "Sorrow in Stone",
Mary, the young Mother gazing in
    grief
at the silent Crucified – in the
    purpose of God, her Son,
Saviour of the World.

Where else can one behold so poignantly
    the deep cost of Mother love?

Harvest Days In Assisi

Problems bruise my mind, but not here –
in Saint Francis's setting, all is as golden
as a slat of sunlight through the door,
as simple as the creatures of God's giving.

Up on the hill, church doors stand open,
the people going with a canticle of praise,
some from village homes in little streets,
some from the far world with eyes of curiosity.

Down here, near the kindly olives,
is the water trough, and at harvest
those faithful to God's earthy purpose
raise the golden stacks and guide the white oxen.

Long, abrasive centuries make no difference,
God's sun rises, and His seasons turn,
cupped in the friendly contour of the hills,
these simple things of the heart live on.

Stepping Into An English Spring

Walking, early, eagerly,
I dismiss Winter with a nod,
now Spring stirs in leaf and bud
over this gentle landscape –
as wide as God's forgiveness,
as eager as Easter morn.
Hope bursts in the least of gardens,
and I hasten to share the Good News,
"Life out of Death, Christ is risen!"

Light In Old London

Born in this century, I missed gas mantles'
    kindly light
till from London's crowded Fleet Street I turned
    towards Temple Church,
tree-hushed, with stone crusaders in their
    chained sleep.

Toward dusk, a figure approached – swift as a moth,
    on a bicycle,
holding aloft an ancient wand for a routine
    task;
and at the very last pole, transferred it to my
    charge.

So hushed, in that hallowed setting, I held my brief
    breath,
and with gathered calm reached up full
    height
to push a hole through the fast-settling darkness –
    a tiny miracle of light!

At A Strange Bus Stop

Does any bus running this way, go there?
I must ask . . .
I should have studied the destination board
Since here I'm a stranger.
Surely there are others wanting
To reach non-stop a Fellowship that really
    works;
To enter into relationships not all tangled
    and knotted tight;
To step off where truth is as clear as a grass-
    stalk silhouetted at dawn;
To stand, at noon, sun-blessed, deeply rooted as
    a spiring pine;

Am I on the right route?
I must ask . . .

Forsaking Tall Cities

I would purify Life's stream – run it through sunlight,
walk between hedges tenanted by clean air,
exchange hard pavements for country paths
and a simple readiness to share.

For landscape marred by machines, God has fresh herbage
to heal hurt suffered by His beloved Earth,
committed to Life, now as ever,
He brings everywhere beauty to birth.

Whit Sunday

Today, I would celebrate God's *kindled flame* –
  with colours blended;
His wind – with feelings given power;
I would adventure forth
  into earth's ways,
with valiant courage, and gentleness,
supporting every living soul with respect,
sending no child loveless to bed.
I would fill my wallet with songs
  that set failures
on their feet in hard places;
I would fling scarves of colour
  across the sordid and the dull,
strengthening wills with purpose
  and clear joy,
sharing the one Gospel.
Love holds its dynamic – Faith and Hope
  rejoicing together –
values of the Young King,
  triumphant as the rapture of lovers,
as dear as one's own name spoken suddenly
  in a strange land!

A Last Day In The English Countryside

I have come back at dusk –
carrying, bee-like, a harvest
from a score of choices –
achievement as modest as a daisy,
praise as high as a lark's song,
laughter as gold as the glory of buttercups!

So this can be counted a rich day –
its panniers packed –
between the first shaft of sunlight
and this kindly hour of sleep!

At The Customs Desk

At last – here I am home – struggling with luggage,
passport, and a fistful of papers all signed!
Moved to mercy, I try not to trouble the officer
with all that I'm smuggling back –
    green fields, and gracious trees established;
    hours of close talk with book-loving friends;
    handsome old buildings, parks and palaces;
    occasional chance nuggets of personal delight;
    sunny turrets; an arrow-head of birds homing at dusk;
    hospitality of many years' making;
    and a dozen welcome pews – on as many Sundays!
But it's late – and I tell myself this courteous officer
is likely to be weary, perhaps, even vexed.
Yet I'm relieved to find ease in pair of tired eyes,
for he picks up his chalk, and scores my case,
with but one word spoken – "Next?"

From Our New
North Shore Home

We who live here, love the winds from
                                    the sea,
fresh each morning,
bringing news of great things into
                                    our lives –
earth and all oceans turning.

Here is no cramping smallness,
                                    but joy
of islands green,
tall yachts flying free across a score
                                    of bays,
trim, sturdy fishing boats far out.

Battered freighters burnished by
                                    obedience,
in storm's percussion,
sharing life with lighthouse keepers,
                                    seabirds,
earth, and all oceans turning!

Nearby Beach

Under sun's canopy of cobalt blue
  within this sickle bay
children dig,
and as confident, at tide's rim,
  gulls, new laundered
strut on orange legs
  as if they own it all.
Here, age-old dangers are dismissed,
  threatening any
bound for distant docks
  with lumbering cranes
like long-necked dinosaurs.

Pensioner

My old neighbour needs to know that she counts:
Sunday she goes to church – and is reassured;
Thursday she goes to town –
climbing aboard the suburban bus, nine o'clock
till three, on a pensioner's pass,
for a few hours holding her handbag,
to look at the shops, and eat a bit of lunch,
with the feeling of being in the flow of humanity,
leaning against the breeze at the crossings,
waiting for the traffic-lights to change –
then on.

My old neighbour stands straighter, taller, on
Sundays and Thursdays.

Any Letters?

Purposefully down the street our postman
                   moves,
his arm in a great gesture of
                   giving,
sowing gladness and grief, life and death
                   in ink,
at each pause among the living.

Countries he knows not, and cities, serve
                   him,
though geography has little to
                   do
with the heart's territories,
                   here,
when his morning's sowing is through.

A Golden Wasp

Sorry, stuttering friend,
   this has shocked you –
meeting with a windscreen
   you can't get through.

Up and down, up and down
   you climb and fall,
frustrated, and now fierce
   on this glass wall.

There are no fresh nectars
   to burgle here –
nothing for a wasp's joy –
   only strange fear.

But I will stop my car –
   Now off you go!
And justly count me "friend".
   You've proved it so!

Storm Prayer

O God – what a night to be out!
The wind sings falsetto all round,
and strong trees thrash their boughs about;
rain has forgotten her kindness
to be a stubborn fury let loose,
beating in anger and blindness.
Have pity, Lord, on the new born,
and aged come to Death's doorstep,
and all creatures but newly shorn.
Bless those boring through dark's despair,
the ill, and all cheated of sleep,
sea-captains, and those in the air;
and support especially this night
all on mercy bent – here and now,
as You lead us through to the new day's
    light.

                                 AMEN

When Sorrow Comes

Not by appointment does one meet Sorrow;
it comes out of the complexities of human belonging –
    swift with dark foreboding – making poorer,
        or richer. Who can say?
    Holding unnoticed silences apart,
        unnoticed contentments,
        it breaks the floodgates
        of one's whole being.
    Easy words slip from one's shoulders
        like a slight shawl;
only Faith in God that goes deep,
        goes deep enough;
        for He has suffered, too,
and alone knows how to heal,
            to sift from grief
                eternal Glory,
                    eternal gain.

Spring's Repeat Performance

This dream of delight never stales –
is no rumour, lovely lie;
Spring's sunshine finds the snow
impatient to be water,
the crocus to don her golden gown,
branch and leaf to speak their lines again.

A repeat performance, but still unsurpassed;
Summer's leafy luxury
waiting in the wings.

Brief Country Visit

Earth's muted orchestra plays on
as I drowse in these waist-tall grasses,
leaving the universe to spin
and the graceful beetle to go up
some slender stalk.

Colours all round just now are cool –
gentlest of greens, browns, and pool-blues,
tall, calm shadows spilling through to
this welcome stillness – with sun's fierce
splinters shut out.

Here is healing for any tired one –
hidden from the traffic of hate
and the hot voices of headlines –
bringing new strength – *when tomorrow
I must go back.*

My Birthday Morning

In crisp colour comes this awaited day –
outside my window
birds are singing as if to split the world;
an hour's summer rain has ceased, and the sun
sends up his golden spears.

Expectation heightens my given joy,
sets my senses on tiptoe,
each day holds hope of something finer,
the brave lark high at his chosen point,
green earth a poem of praise!

Let Me Be Aware!

O Lord, let me be aware –
    quicken my heart to care
for Your world; and each holding breath
    cast between Birth and Death –
birds, at first light, greeting the day
    before small winds can say
what can be said of Life's wonder
    here inexhaustible:

And Earth's furry things on four feet,
    always subject to cold and heat,
and wild vagaries of delight
    hidden to human sight;
even to children with unpatterned Time,
    astir with song and rhyme
and Life's bright curiosities
    here inexhaustible:

All who work with moods of Earth –
    that give fruits and grains birth,
twigs and buds foliate joy;
    and all whose main ploy
is cast with Life's indoor things –
    the desk, and bell that rings,
or the lab's vast awe of the Atom,
    here inexhaustible:

All with fresh healing skills to bring,
  all with glad songs to sing,
all whose words set men on their feet
  with news that God will greet
them on their way through Time and Space
  with His forgiveness and Grace,
incarnate in Christ's great glory.
  Here inexhaustible!

A Scrap Of Country News

This morning brought me a miracle –
a mild Jersey cow in a coat of velvet,
quietly chewing her cud by the flowering hawthorn – a web
delicately spun between two slender twigs outstretched,
with transparent globules of silver, there
set by the world's Supreme Jeweller.

Hushed, my heart accepted this beauty – as if Time,
in the haste of man's ways, had no pressure on me;
since the Creator of galaxies far out, above solid earth,
must know better than any, what Life is all about.
A simple man learned it once, in the space of Horeb's desert,
turning from minding sheep, to hush his heart before a burning
bush.*

*Exodus 3:1–5

One Old Pensioner

She owned the smallest garden
as proud hostess to the sun;
and passers-by gazed always
at one red geranium.

She had no book to teach her;
but Love served her from the start,
and showers, and bees, faithful,
mastered many things by heart.

That tiny street spoke God's joy
throughout many sun-filled hours –
shared by those in His employ,
and one potful of red flowers.

Trees

Our Lord of Nazareth loved trees,
as He grew – and needed them
for His daily privacy at prayer,
as continually for His craft
at His village bench.
Men with daily needs sought Him
to make things and to mend.
And His skills never failed them,
nor His knowledge of wood's strength and grain.
Later, about the business
of God's gracious Kingdom,
He judged the beautiful grain
and staying power of men and women.

Monday Morning Early!

Cock-crow splinters stars across sleep –
Dawn whitens its knuckles on
                              shutters;
Dreams surrender a kindly hold.
But there is no escape for me –
I must stir to this lively call.

In all too short a time, the Sun
will gather Westward its fine
                              gold –
rejoicing in an offered peace –
And I will seek out a loved book,
Or write off a letter I owe.

Night may bring cares for tomorrow,
that hinders acceptance of Sleep.
                    Though –
I will not hesitate long;
My Life comes in God's great design,
As His first gift – *a day at a time* . . .

I Am A Traveller Too!

To think that now
I can head my letters home "Vienna", "Florence", "Rome",
each alive with beauty and song,
patterns yet incomplete –
save only in heart beat.

Inquisitive sun slants
through spacious and small streets, as I move
snatching at history's splendours,
where also grim deeds hide –
courage, and ugly pride.

These all clamour for space
on my page, "coax my heart to my sleeve",
things of life and death to share
with the folk back home –
headed proudly "Vienna", "Florence", "Rome".

Leisure

Life's clamour of city streets
beats hard upon the soul,
without many green places
to make one whole.
As where living trees
lift their heads on high,
and a lark goes up with song
into the blue sky.
Only where Love is the measure
and things are clearly seen,
with Praise as pure as God's Presence,
is the grass truly green.

Shining Miracle

Call it "a miracle", as you have chosen.
You took time off from daily living
to save your life;
and in hospital, medical skills
gathered through the centuries
came to your aid, as if you were the only one
that moment in need.

No one asked about your human worth –
though I knew it well, after years
and tests no hospital takes.
No one asked about politics,
or the essence of your education.
To you, my friend, *costly co-operation*
came offering, without stint, precious gifts.

But hasn't this long been God's
way with miracles?

Love's Secrets

As fresh as this morning's dew,
As old as the Moon,
And close to me and you,
To be realized soon.

As clean as a wood flame,
As free as the air,
As gallant as a game,
As graceful and fair.

As high as the Pleiades,
As deep as human pain,
As natural as ease
When dusk comes again.

This is Love – each hour
For us, high and low,
And nothing else has power
To rejoice us so!

Builders

They mortared their bricks with pride,
those old-time builders of Babel* –
and their tower grasping to high heaven
collapsed in wretched confusion.

This known, I would build up my Tower
from a quarry well-tested by time –
of Laughter, Love, Courage,
Forgiveness, and commonplace Joy!

*Genesis 11:3–9

Winter Always Has To Give In

Our shining streets just now are scrubbed
   and rinsed with rain.
Daffodils soberly beneath the soil, have
   not yet broken through –
But they will!

This is God's world, and He is wholly
   committed to Life!
Darkness and Chaos surrendered to Him, in the
   crisis of Creation;
And centuries on – in Calvary's Garden of
   Grief.

Fearful disciples hid behind slammed doors.
One, already hung on the Judas-tree; and Thomas
   was sadly wrapped in his doubts,
But God's heart was wholly centred – as still –
   on "A Stone Rolled Away" –
And the glory of Life!

At The End Of Years

When I reach old age, let me recall
the green delights and pains of childhood –
small leaf patterns dancing on a wall,
wasp- and bee-stings never understood,
and sweet chestnut's candelabra.

Let the brisk ambitious cock still crow,
and laggard senses be roused at dawn –
with all that Time has helped me to know
in the crowded years since I was born,
to share the height and depth of living.

The Eternal Salient in Time
makes such things meaningful evermore –
God's rich gifts amidst prose and rhyme,
opening at last, Death's hingèd door
to an experience of Life unguessed!

The Godwits Go

Alighting a moment on the sea-flats
of salty Manukau,
they gather from far –
departing guests of our grazing acres,
in swift flight,
as countless others before them –
set on emigration.

A thousand wings resting –
now they make ready to leave
for far Siberia –
nine thousand man-reckoned air miles
in response to an urge –
the "Iron Curtain" of modern making
nothing to them.

Year by year, others come – and
gathering together, go,
birds of two worlds, small
feathered adventurers:
"Two worlds are ours", I, too, hold in my heart,
though this glory is lost to many today
in earth's clamour.

As silently I stand alone gazing
till nothing is left to my eyes
save Manukau's sea-flats
and this precious moment to remind me
of Albrecht Dürer's shared Faith
given a place on his gravestone,
Emigravi! – gone!

Born Rich

A breath brought me
into this inheritance, speaking the syllables of Time –
to little green beetles rapturously climbing
slender grass stalks,
bees in velvet, murmuring,
paths made by other feet across friendly fields,
hills laced with leisure,
with hints only of the dark spaces
between my stars.

All purpose then
was in an hour, all Summer in a flower –
weed patterns in the mill waters,
quick minnows playing
their hide-and-seek, mocking time and care;
soil's primal delight
sending the plough down the furrow,
merging work and hope, white gulls
following after.

Seed flung widely
with a gesture of great giving
was answered by silver rain –
and young spears of green,
at season's end, golden
to the glory of God and man –
all hands and hours then filled,
cart horses and men at midday seeking shade
beside soaring stacks.

Till birth brought me,
how could I know all this awaited –
the hiss of scythe,
whirr of hone sharpening the long blade,
and morning by morning, a thrush singing
from a favourite tree-top;
"Get up, get!
Be quick, be quick, be quick!
Stick to it, stick to it!"

Never now
shall I fear to surrender breath to Him
who made these things –
marrying lightning's jagged jewel to thunder,
rapturous joy to pain,
bringing Life out of Death –
that beyond, clothed anew,
I may look again on my beloved,
with awed recognition!

Also available in Fount Paperbacks

BOOKS BY RITA SNOWDEN

Discoveries That Delight

'Thirty brief chapters of reflections on selected psalms . . . The
book is very readable. Its style has been achieved through many
years of work to produce a vehicle of religious communication
with a wide appeal.'

Neville Ward, Church of England Newspaper

Further Good News

'Another enjoyable book from Rita Snowden; easy to read and
with a store of good things to ponder over and store in the mind.
The author shows clearly that there is much Good News in our
world and that this is very much the gift of a loving God.'

Church Army Review

I Believe Here and Now

'Once again she has produced for us one of the most readable and
helpful pieces of Christian witness I have seen . . .'

D. P. Munro, Life and Work

A Woman's Book of Prayer

'This book will make prayer more real and meaningful for all who
use it. There is all through the book an accent of reality. Here the
needs of the twentieth century are brought to God in twentieth
century language.'

William Barclay

More Prayers for Women

'. . . she has that rare and valuable gift of being able to compose
forms of prayer which really do express the aspirations of many
people . . .'

Philip Cecil, Church Times

Fount Paperbacks

Fount is one of the leading paperback publishers of religious books and below are some of its recent titles.

- THE WAY OF ST FRANCIS Murray Bodo £2.50
- GATEWAY TO HOPE Maria Boulding £1.95
- LET PEACE DISTURB YOU Michael Buckley £1.95
- DEAR GOD, MOST OF THE TIME YOU'RE QUITE NICE Maggie Durran £1.95
- CHRISTIAN ENGLAND VOL 3 David L Edwards £4.95
- A DAZZLING DARKNESS Patrick Grant £3.95
- PRAYER AND THE PURSUIT OF HAPPINESS Richard Harries £1.95
- THE WAY OF THE CROSS Richard Holloway £1.95
- THE WOUNDED STAG William Johnston £2.50
- YES, LORD I BELIEVE Edmund Jones £1.75
- THE WORDS OF MARTIN LUTHER KING Coretta Scott King (Ed) £1.75
- BOXEN C S Lewis £4.95
- THE CASE AGAINST GOD Gerald Priestland £2.75
- A MARTYR FOR THE TRUTH Grazyna Sikorska £1.95
- PRAYERS IN LARGE PRINT Rita Snowden £2.50
- AN IMPOSSIBLE GOD Frank Topping £1.95
- WATER INTO WINE Stephen Verney £2.50

All Fount paperbacks are available at your bookshop or newsagent, or they can be ordered by post from Fount Paperbacks, Cash Sales Department, G.P.O. Box 29, Douglas, Isle of Man, British Isles. Please send purchase price, plus 15p per book, maximum postage £3. Customers outside the U.K. send purchase price, plus 15p per book. Cheque, postal or money order. No currency.

NAME (Block letters) —————————————————————

ADDRESS ——————————————————————————————

——————————————————————————————————————